The Rich Fool

Illustrations by Derek Matthews

CHRISTIAN FOCUS PUBLICATIONS

Jesus told a story about a man who was greedy.

A rich farmer had a very good harvest.

'What can I do?' he thought. 'I haven't anywhere to keep my corn.'

Then he had an idea. 'I know,' he said.
'I will tear down my barns...'

'...and build BIGGER ones!'

'Then I can store my corn *and* all my other goods.'

'I will have everything I need to last for many years.'

'I will eat good food, drink and enjoy
myself.'

What a selfish man!

He didn't think to share his riches.
And he didn't think about God.

'You fool!' said God. 'Tonight you are going to die.'

'Now who will get all these things you
have kept to yourself?'

God loves us to thank him for the things He gives us.

He is pleased when we share them with others.

God does not want us to store up
riches like the greedy farmer. He will
look after those who trust in Him.

This story can be found in the Bible in
Luke 12: 13 - 21